Paris 1899

First published in 2001 by Newmarket Press, New York

This edition published 2001 by FilmFour Books, an imprint of Pan Macmillan Ltd, Pan Macmillan, 20 New Wharf Road, London N1 9RR, Basingstoke and Oxford.

Associated companies throughout the world

www.panmacmillan.com

ISBN 0 7522 61940

9 8 7 6 5 4 3 2 1

A CIP catalogue record for this book is available from the British Library.

COVER DESIGN: SILVANA AZZI, ALEXANDRA BOLTON & CATHERINE MARTIN
PREVIOUS PAGE PARIS 1899: SIMON WHITELEY, ANDY BROWN, IAN BROWN, DAVID DULAC, BRETT FEENAY, LINDSAY FLEAY AND AIDAN SARSFIELD, ANIMAL LOGIC
THIS PAGE EXTERIOR MOULIN ROUGE COLLAGE: BAZMARK DESIGN

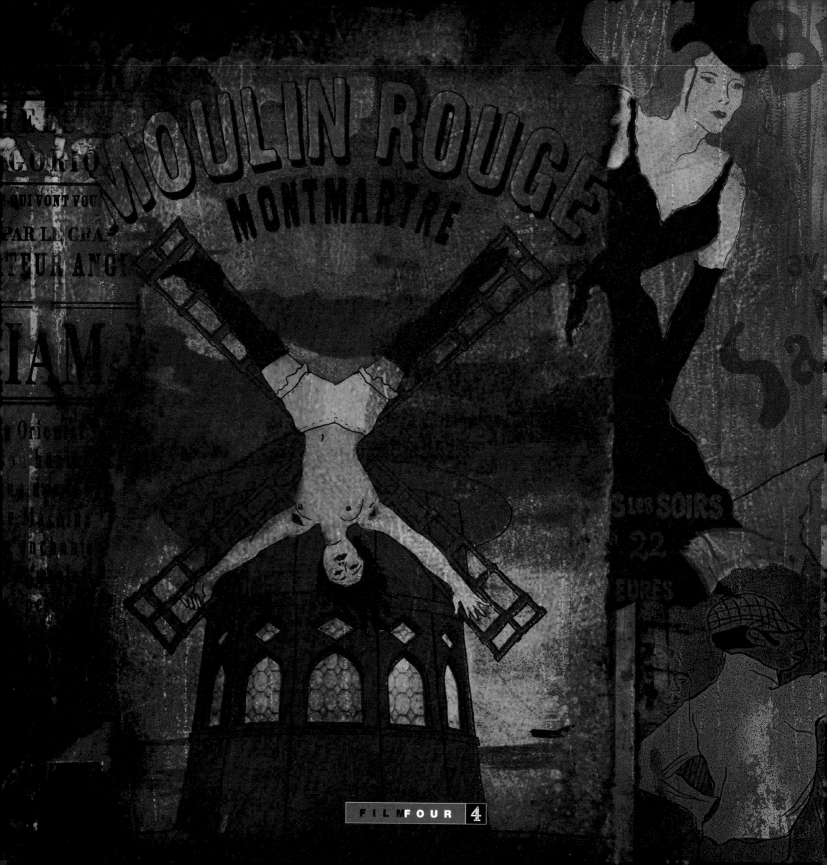

CM AND I SAT IN THE GIGANTIC AUDITORIUM OF AN 'ICECREAM PALACE' CINEMA IN RAJASTHAN, INDIA.

ALONG WITH A COUPLE OF THOUSAND CINEMA-GOING LOCALS STARING UP AT THE SCREEN

I EXPERIENCED MY FIRST 'BOLLYWOOD MUSICAL'. THE FILM SWUNG EFFORTLESSLY FROM SLAPSTICK

HUMOUR AND HINDI POP SONG SEQUENCES TO CONFRONTING VIOLENCE AND MOVING TRAGEDY.

THREE HOURS PASSED EASILY, PINNED TO OUR SEATS WATCHING A FILM IN A FOREIGN LANGUAGE WITH

NO SUBTITLES. AFTER SEEING THAT FILM I WAS LEFT WITH THE UNDERSTANDING THAT THE BOLLYWOOD

MUSICAL AND ITS OUTRAGEOUS COMIC TRAGIC STORYTELLING SUCCEEDED BECAUSE OF A DEAL THAT EXISTS

BETWEEN THE FILM AND ITS AUDIENCE. IN THIS ARRANGEMENT THE PRETENCE THAT WHAT IS TO BE

EXPERIENCED IS IN ANY WAY *REAL* IS SWEPT AWAY. THE AUDIENCE IS CONSTANTLY MADE AWARE THAT THEY

ARE ALWAYS WATCHING A FILM, NOT REALITY. MOREOVER, THEY ARE INVITED TO PARTICIPATE, HENCE THE

LOUD REACTIONS AND TALKING AT THE SCREEN AS IF THEY WERE AT A LIVE THEATRE SHOW. I FELT THE FILM

WAS A DISTANT COUSIN TO OUR FIRST FILM *STRICTLY BALLROOM*. IT WAS A KIND OF THEATRICALISED

CINEMA BUT THIS INDIAN FILM WASN'T JUST MUSICAL COMEDY IT WAS EQUAL PART TRAGEDY. AT THE END,

AS WE WANDERED OFF INTO THE WARM INDIAN NIGHT I THOUGHT TO MYSELF: COULD A CONTRACT LIKE THIS

BE STRUCK WITH AN AUDIENCE IN THE WEST? THAT WAS SEVEN YEARS AGO...

Moulin Rouge is the third feature in a style we've dubbed the 'Red Curtain' trilogy. A theatricalised cinema style we launched with *Strictly Ballroom*, developed with *Romeo+Juliet*, and intend to complete with *Moulin Rouge*. The 'Red Curtain' style that defines our filmmaking thus far comprises several distinct storytelling rules and parameters. A simple even naive story based on a primary myth is set in a heightened interpretation of a world that is at once familiar yet distant and exotic. Think of the world of ballroom dancing in *Strictly*, the postmodern Verona Beach in *Romeo+Juliet* or the luminous underworld that is the *Moulin Rouge*. Finally, each of the 'Red Curtain' trilogy has a device which awakens the audience to the experience of watching the film rather than putting them

of what was originally a very raw and shocking dance, the can-can. Our *Moulin Rouge*, in which we hope to recreate for audiences now the thrill of what was sensationally seedy to the punters then. That is: big, sexy, straight off the boulevards and illuminated by that modern miracle the electric lightbulb to excessively kitschy effect. The nightclub of your dreams. A place where you could dance, watch a show and have sex with the participants – or at least be teased by the prospect of such. That's the experience myself and Bazmark collaborators, both old and new, have sunk our collective creative energy and wit into making real. To be clear, the whole stylistic premise has been to decode what the Moulin Rouge was to the audiences of 1899 and express

nothing can change that, then that's also a reflection of the change I've undergone in recent years. Nor is it stretching a point to remark that *Moulin*'s Boho (i.e. Bohemian) gang of four, dreaming and rehearsing their show-within-a-show 'Spectacular Spectacular' in Toulouse-Lautrec's studio and their whole vexed relationship to 'the money' (embodied by that most conditional of investors, the Duke) makes play with our often equally comically beleaguered process. Commercial Bohemianism, you could call it – near oxymoron that it is. Certainly during the near-epic staging and filming of Montmartre, Paris, on ten immodestly lush sets in Sydney, Australia, I have asked myself do I strategically set up House of Iona, the production house where Bazmark lives

WE SHARE THE BOHO'S NAIVE BELIEF IN TRUTH, FREEDOM, BEAUTY AND LOVE

into a dream state. In *Strictly Ballroom* the key scenes are told through dance. In *Romeo+Juliet* it was Shakespeare's heightened 400-year-old language. In *Moulin Rouge*, our ultimate 'Red Curtain' gesture, the audience are awakened by the experience of music, song and dance. 'A musical' I hear you say. Yes, perhaps a pop opera or a people's opera or a comi-tragi music film. An attempt at re-inventing an old tradition in a new form, dangerous, full of risks, if it works the naming of genre will happen later. *Moulin Rouge*, with a plot born of the Orphean myth and moulded in the likeness of a tragic 19th century novel, Dumas' 'Camille' or Zola's 'Nana', is set in a heightened interpretation of end-of-century Paris seen through a very contemporary lens, a shockingly operatic, high pop, high camp kind of lens. It's our own *Moulin Rouge*, with an ecstatic refit

that same thrill in a way that our contemporary moviegoers can relate to. On a more personal note, *Moulin Rouge* is my love-letter to a hard graft lesson: you can't live for opening night alone. This in spite of the fact that we at Bazmark are veritable slaves to that deliriously many-armed god. In fact our hero Christian's journey, modelled on the mythic descent of Orpheus into the underworld, is twinned not just by my own journey but perhaps by all of us here at Bazmark. To be frank, I selected the Orpheus myth because I wanted to tell a story about growing up, and about the need to travel through and pass beyond the underworld in order to do so. And if *Moulin Rouge* culminates for Ewan McGregor's Christian, in that moment when you realise there are things bigger than yourself, some relationships cannot last, people will die, you will get older and

and works, and then do *Moulin Rouge*: a bent reflection of the Bazmark band of lunatics...Or does it happen by osmosis? The truth is, both. CM (Catherine Martin) and I, plus the core collaborators on this film, in some crucial sense live in a kind of Moulin Rouge. We share the Boho's naive belief in Truth, Freedom, Beauty and Love. And like our courtesan and poet lovers Satine and Christian, like impresario Zidler and Toulouse's improvisatory band of Bohos, we're constantly dealing with the intersection of our ideals with the harsh reality of time and economics. Art, sex, commerce – and hair...the nexus of *Moulin Rouge's* story on-camera and off. Suffice to say that the sex-for-sale business that keeps the sails of the Moulin Rouge turning, with Satine the consummate vendor, is also the world of show business where illusion and performance prevail.

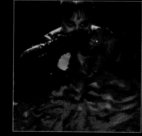

CHAPTER 6

CHAPTER 7

CHAPTER 8

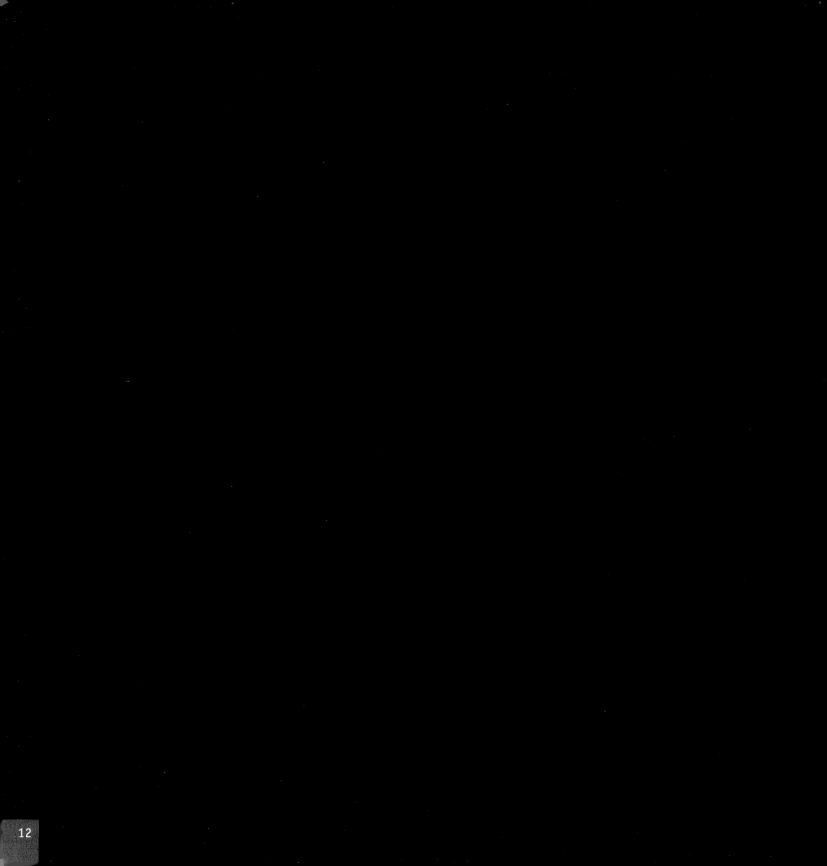

This is a story
about love.
Love overcomi...
obstacles

THIS IS
A STORY
ABOUT
LOVE

PHOTOGRAPHY BY SUE ADLER

1

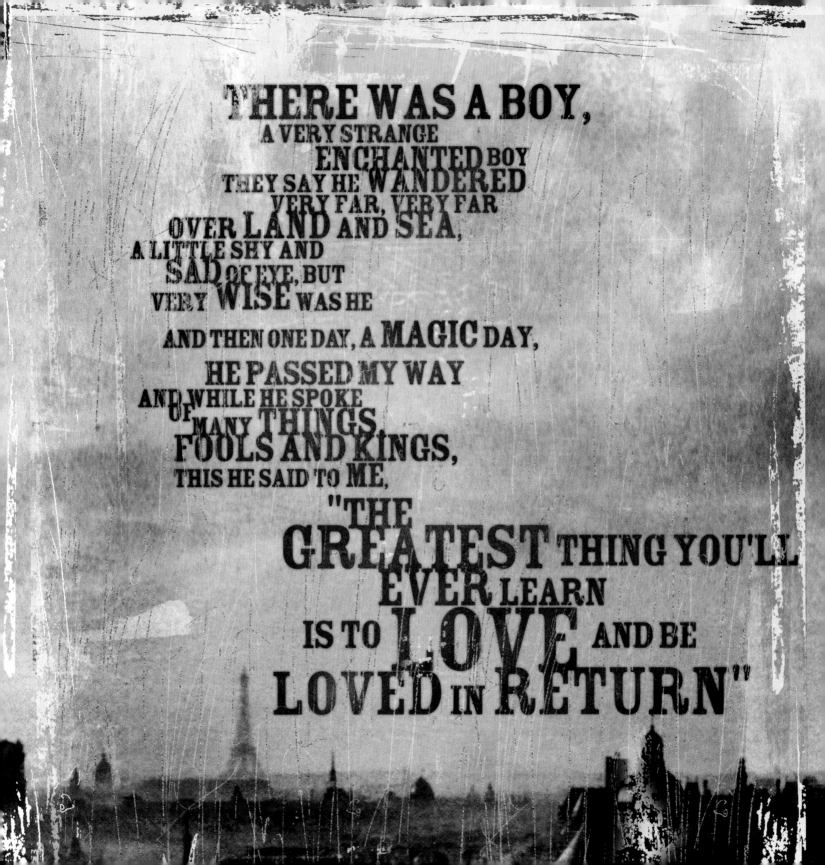

Toulouse whispers:
It's her. The Sparkling Diamond.

Cut to: The cold beady eyes of the Duke.
He watches Satine intently.

Topographical Shot:
The hats tilt back in unison
gaze upon the unearthly vision
the jewel encrusted Sparkling Diamond.
A deep, hot silence fills the hall.

Satine: Let's Dance

Christian: I'd prefer to do it standing

Satine: Show me your poetry

Satine: On opening night

I'm going to sleep with the Duke.

Duke: You made me believe you loved me.
Well... I might as well get what I came for.

The chorus chants
with demonic intensity.

Satine: Tell our story Christian, that way
we'll always be together

A final breath,
Satine:... the show must go on...

OPEN TO: MELANCHOLIC STRINGS. A BEAUTIFULLY HAND-WRITTEN CARD. IT READS: 'PARIS 1899'. SUPER OVER: A SEPIA TONED VISTA OF TURN-OF-THE-CENTURY PARIS. THE EIFFEL TOWER VAULTS SKYWARD. IN THE DISTANCE A SOLITARY HILL IS CROWNED WITH A HALF-CONSTRUCTED CATHEDRAL. A RAMSHACKLE LITTLE VILLAGE AT THE BASE OF THE HILL NOW COMES INTO VIEW. SUPER: 'MONTMARTRE'. PUSH TOWARDS: AN UNPREPOSSESSING GARRET.

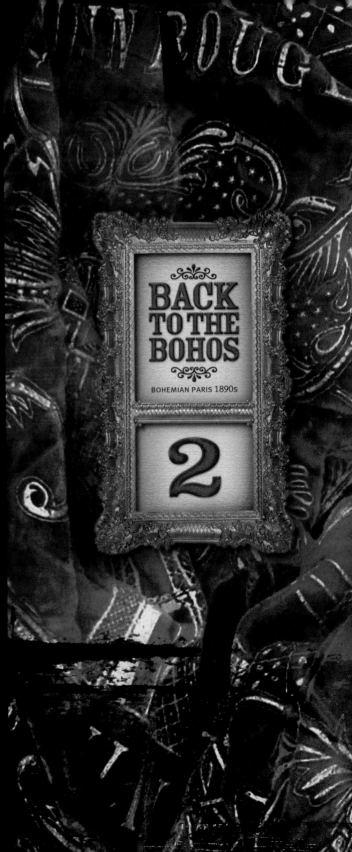

BACK TO THE BOHOS

BOHEMIAN PARIS 1890s

2

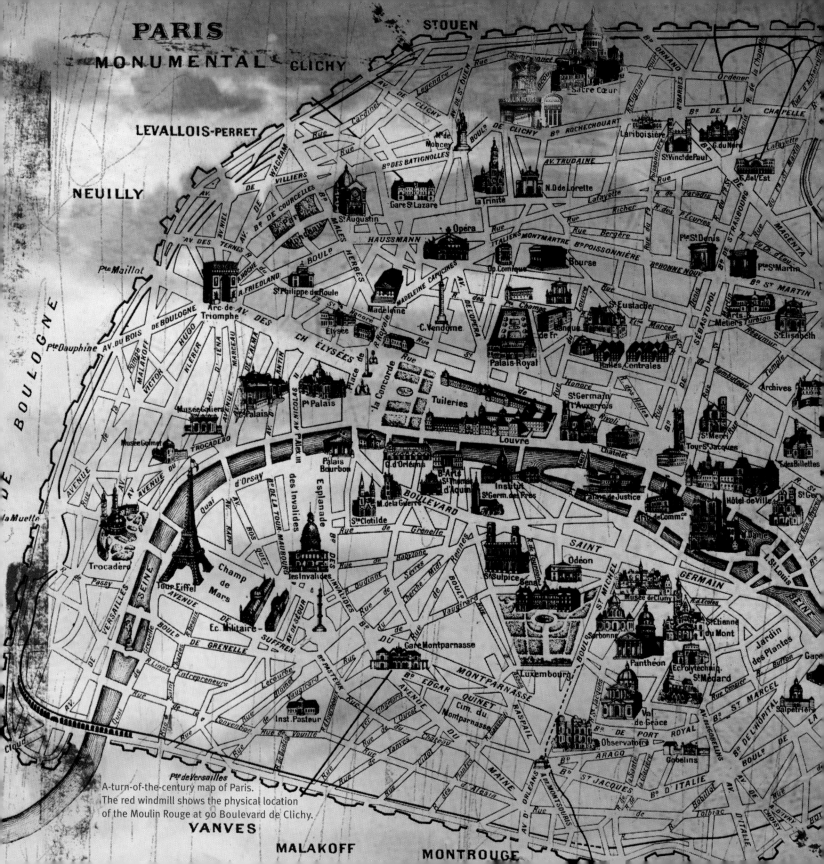

A turn-of-the-century map of Paris.
The red windmill shows the physical location
of the Moulin Rouge at 90 Boulevard de Clichy.

IN THE CLOSING DECADE OF NINETEENTH CENTURY
PARIS A NEW PERIOD RETROSPECTIVELY CHRISTENED
'LA BELLE EPOQUE' (THE BEAUTIFUL PERIOD)
WAS BORN. AS ITS NAME SUGGESTS, THE BELLE EPOQUE
WAS CHARACTERISED BY RELATIVE CALM, PROSPERITY,
ENTERPRISE AND SOCIAL FREEDOM.

Most importantly for our story, the Belle Epoque gave birth to a new culture of entertainments immediately recognisable as modern. To mark the centenary of the French Revolution, a revolution against privilege and inequity, Paris staged the Universal Exhibition of 1889. Here, a variety of amusements and new technologies serviced wondrous worker and bourgeois alike. This 'levelling of enjoyments' as one contemporary called it, marked a democratisation of leisure that heralded the 20th century's invention of mass culture. As Paris raced toward the end of the century, automation and mass production brought heady rewards. There was more bread, wine, books, textiles, fashionable garments and new concept Parisian department stores to buy them in. Above all, the populace made a dizzying start on the 20th century's love affair with new technologies.

ILLUSTRATION: CONCEPT FOR MATTE PAINTING OF PARIS BY GRANT FRECKELTON AND ANDY BROWN AT ANIMAL LOGIC.

The
invention of the
telegraph, the telephone, the
elevator, the bicycle, hand-held cameras,
the first automobiles, the electric light and
the first mass produced typewriters – not to mention
advances in both public hygiene and in surgery – led to
an optimism at once practical and utopian. For the
Bohemians of Montmartre, who in our story called themselves
'the Children of the Revolution', the promise of 'Truth, Beauty,
Freedom and Love!', of a better world, seemed germane in these
unprecedented new technologies. But it wasn't all unalloyed
progress and joy. Along with the benefits of the machine age came
bitter social dilemmas. Paris drank as never before, increasingly as
a social past-time, spawning a new social disease: alcoholism.
Tuberculosis, organised prostitution, the spread of syphilis, and
overcrowding, as the promise of regular income beckoned those
from farming communities to the ever-swelling cities, abounded.
Still, evidence of a new mood afoot is wittily immortalised in a
contemporary pamphlet attacking the work ethic and the
misery of workers in capitalist industry – and entitled 'The
Right to be Lazy'. Here, author Lafarge condemns the
'dogma of work', chastises French workers for
'vegetating in abstinence' and recommends
work be confined by law to three hours a
day in favour of a new healthful
'regime of laziness'.

With the rise of organised mass labour came the new concept of 'leisure hours' and a demand for mass entertainments. A booming middle class found more time for distraction – and more money to spend on it. An ever-growing new demand for popular entertainment, for race tracks, circuses, opera, brothels, cabarets and balls, was voiced. Indeed, turn-of - the-century Paris hosted some 27,000 cafes which, in tandem with the wine bars and cabarets, gave it more drinking places than any other city in the world. By century's end, 264 cafe-concerts or 'theatres of the poor', many of which evolved into their grander relation, the music and dance hall, also flourished. Here, bourgeois, worker and Bohemian alike could enjoy a song or a theatrical act for the price of a drink. All kind of distractions were in vogue, and the low life, in particular the amorous low life, was suddenly hot. Located right in the heart of artistic Bohemia and Paris' criminal underworld, the establishments of the Montmartre district were perfectly equipped to serve it up...and to fulfil that yen which the French even coined a phrase for, that is 'la nostalgie de la boue' (lit: longing for mud).

Crowning the Montmartre-based world of commercial entertainment was Joseph Oller and Charles Zidler's landmark music hall, the Moulin Rouge. When the Moulin Rouge opened its doors on the Place Blanche at the foot of Montmartre on the 6th of October 1889, all Paris turned out. Highbrow and lowbrow society alike mobbed the 'Palace of Women' before the paintwork was dry on its extravagantly decorated interior. The Moulin Rouge's decor, by Montmartre painter Adolphe Willette, its exotic colour, form and themeing became an overnight legend. Besides the immense dance hall complete with galleries to watch the dance floor and an orchestra mounted above the stage, there was a garden with another stage, cafe tables, cavorting monkeys and un-stockinged prostitutes riding donkeys. Also in the garden, a giant elephant (gleaned when the Universal Exhibition of 1889 terminated, housed an Arabian-themed club inside its body. Male clients entered via the elephant's leg where a spiral staircase opened onto belly dancing performances, an orchestra and an opium den. Making a radical break with the century's relentless class divisions, a microcosm of Parisian society rubbed shoulders in scandalous proximity. European royalty (including the Prince of

Wales), ambassadors, politicians, industrialists and magistrates slummed it with celebrity courtesans, can-can girls and workers. The local Montmartre Bohemians and the cocottes and noctambules (prostitutes),pimps, madams and thieves who were their neighbours were also out in force. Within the Moulin's velvet draped walls, the aromas of women's scent, face powder, tobacco and beer mingled as

promiscuously as the audience. In a class of their own were the courtesans, a social phenomena that all but died out with the end of the Belle Epoque and the beginning of World War I. Though springing from the same working class as the prostitutes, the more celebrated courtesans were distinguished by the length and high-style of the relation-ships they formed (with, near exclusively the elite of Europe).

Like today's film stars and super-models, they were also cultishly observed by press and public. But if the Moulin Rouge quickly established its reputation as the most exotic sex market in Paris, it also represented a kind of cultural and social revolution. Think of it as a can-can besotted version of Steve Rubell's disco-crazed Studio 54 crossed with Bangkok's sex market meets Mardi Gras' carnival.

The Bohemian's anti-establishment mores thrived in Mont-martre, whose Butte district was honeycombed with the studios of struggling, long-haired poets, painters, sculptors, musicians and students. Shunning the bourgeois world of their parents generation, the Bohemians plunged into cafe society, leftist ideologies and a drug and alcohol culture that many – notably the legendary poet Rimbaud and his lover Verlaine – saw as the gateway to artistic inspiration and transcendence. With characteristically anarchistic verve, Bohemian artists broke with the ultra conservative Academies and took art to the streets with their posters, overnight magazines, satiric cabarets, costume balls and the democratise theatre of the cafe-concerts. Painters began to observe the demimonde – t streetwalkers, beggars, drunks and petty crims they cohabited amongst – with a frankne and an observational wit that challenged establishment mores. Artist Henri de Toulou Lautrec, reluctant scion of one of France's oldest aristocratic houses, became one of the m notorious Bohemians of fin-de-siècle Montmartre. (At 4'11 – a genetic bone condition h stunted his growth – he was also one of the shortest.) Lautrec immortalised th inhabitants of bar, brothel and dance hall in his paintings, prints and posters with a stylishly simplified perspective that is now credited as one of the earliest forms of visual Modernism. Lautrec, whom a contemporary described as 'a queer top heavy little man, swaying on his stunted legs like a ship at sea', was a favourite at the Moulin Rouge with management and dancers alike. Armed with his legendary wit and drafting skills, and a fashionably fatal alcoholic habit, the diminutive Frenchman partied and observed the world from his regular table, often till dawn.

THE ABSINTHE
THE MYTHICAL
'GREEN FAIRY'

LA GOULUE:
THE ORIGINAL
HIGH PRIESTESS
OF CAN-CAN, A
DANCER AND
POSER FROM THE
MOULIN ROUGE.

CHA-U-KAO: A CLOWN AND ACROBAT AT THE MOULIN
ROUGE WHO WAS NAMED WITH AN ORIENTAL VERSION
OF 'CHAHUT-CHAOS', A TERM GIVEN TO THE
WILD DANCES OF THE TIME.

Entertainments at the Moulin
Rouge included roaming performers and
sideshow freaks; witty social comedy and stand-
up; an opportunity to listen to the latest Edison
phonograph from New York; a view of Paris from the howdah
atop the Elephant or somewhere deep in its belly; a quiet shot of
morphine; pseudo-exotic dancers; every sexual favour or deviance
imaginable for a price; and most famously, the can-can dancers.
Evolved in Paris' ragingly popular cafe-concerts and music halls, and
identified with the lower classes, the can-can's violent abandonment and
erotic acrobatics were the sensation of the day. Considered especially
provocative was the height and violence of the dancers' leg kicks which
were literally policed via the safety pinning of their split panties.
Legendary can-can practitioners at the Moulin Rouge included Jane Avril,
La Goulue (lit: the Glutton, named for her habit of draining abandoned
glasses at the bar) and the male dancer Valentin Le Desosse
(the Boneless)...all of whom were favoured by Toulouse-Lautrec.
There was also Nini Pattes-en-l'air (Nini-Legs-in-
the-Air) and Mome Fromage, a plump lesbian
red-head. Inspiring further characters
in the film were the North
African cabaret artist
Le Chocolat and
the curious Le
Petomane,
a musical
farter

THE
MOULIN ROUGE
IS THE HIGH TEMPLE
OF DEGRADATION
AND HUMAN PERVERSION

DANCERS AND PIN-UPS FROM THE MOULIN ROUGE: LEFT, THE ORIGINAL MÔME FROMAGE OR "CHEESE KID", BELOW THE ORIGINAL NINI-PATTES-EN-L'AIR OR "NINI-LEGS-IN-THE-AIR".

CAN-CAN COHORTS: LA GOULUE OR "THE GLUTTON", NICKNAMED FOR DRAINING THE DREGS OF ALCOHOL FROM GLASSES AT THE MOULIN ROUGE AND GRILLE D'ÉGOUT OR "SEWER GRATE", KNOWN FOR HER GAPPY TEETH.

AT THE MOULIN ROUGE BY TOULOUSE-LAUTREC 1895. GASLIGHT AND ABSINTHE RESULTED IN THE GREENISH HUE OF LAUTREC'S SUBJECTS.

RÉGIANE, SPOOFED BY ANNA HELD AND MALLET AS A "DELICIOUS BURLESQUE" IN: "THE MOULIN ROUGE REVUE".

whose 'aspiratory anus' caused corseted ladies to be carried out in breathless hilarity. The cocktail of choice among cabaret and musical hall goers was a bitter green alcohol called Absinthe that had something of a cult following amongst the Bohemians. With a high spirit content, absinthe also contained elements of the poisonous herb wormwood and had rumoured hallucinogenic qualities. Its popularity in late 19th century Paris inspired a renaming of the city's beloved cocktail hour to l'heure verte, or 'green hour'. Taken either with or without sugar, absinthe inspired one Parisian poet to shout "I take it with sugar" as a rapturous form of greeting that sorted fellow users from non.

ONCE YOU ENTER THERE IS NO ESCAPE

SUPER CLOSE: ZIDLER SLOWLY TURNS, THE SIGN THAT READS MOULIN ROUGE INCARNATING THE MAGIC WORDS THAT APPEAR. ZIDLER (SINGS) THE CAN-CAN! THE SCREEN EXPLODES INTO CAN-CAN CHAOS AS DOZENS OF EXOTICALLY COSTUMED FEMALE DANCERS, SKIRTS HELD HIGH, THRASH THROUGH THE MAIN HALL OF THE MOULIN ROUGE WITH DEATH-DEFYING PHYSICAL ABANDON.

YOU CAN CAN-CAN

BUMP 'N' GRIND

3

The notion of entrepreneurs stealing shocking, sexy, working-class dance crazes from their natural environs and putting them into naughty-but-nice palaces of pleasure for the rich to participate in a little slumming is nothing new. Steve Rubell and Ian Schrager's Studio 54 and its disco craze is a perfect example. In the 1890s the dangerous working - class street dance was called the can-can.The dance evolved out of the high-kicking underwear-flashing polkas of Parisian music halls of the 1840s, through the quadrille and the chahut to find its final outrage-topping form in the can-can. Originating with male

THE ESTABLISHMENT-THUMBING,

SEX-FLASHING DANCE CRAZE

dancers who launched into flying splits that gave the can-can its ecstatic conclusion. By the time the can-can reached its zenith at the Moulin Rouge, it had become a provocatively female preserve with male dancers the exception rather than the rule. The sex-flashing dance craze, the can-can, practised by working-class/working girls turned professional dancers made Montmartre's Moulin Rouge the funkiest place to slum it from 1889 on. Here was a dance whose standard moves – the practised petticoat manipulation, the suspender/thigh flash, the high kicks and the final grand ecart (or splits) – allowed individual dancers the wildest of

HERE WAS

A DANCE

THAT ALLOWED

INDIVIDUALS

THE WILDEST OF

IMPROVISATIONS,

THE COOLEST OF

INDECENCIES.

Right: The can-can: bottoms up!
PHOTO BY SUE ADLER

improvisations, the coolest of indecencies and had the spectator reeling at their lack of underwear or glimpse of split panties. In fact there was an inspector called Le Pere Pudeur (the Father of Decency) who patrolled dance halls of the time and supposedly ensured the dancers' modesty. One of the most famous historical can-can dancers (subject of many of Toulouse-Lautrec's paintings) was La Goulue (the glutton) a washerwoman's daughter who gained her moniker by indiscriminately finishing any unattended glasses at the bars and clubs she frequented. La Goulue (photo pg 52) became a millionaire through her charm, extra-ordinary dancing and the favours of her many male admirers. (Sadly, she finished life as an alcoholic selling peanuts to passers-by outside the Moulin Rouge after a disastrous business venture involving a lion-taming sideshow.) Acrobatic skill, agility and devil-may-care passion were valued over mere prettiness. Practitioners free-formed into erotic dervishes, walked on their hands and kicked off the top hats of bystanders whose overheated faces pushed too close, or dragged the same men into dance in an act of violently exciting class-levelling extraordinary for its day. Most revolutionary of all: the defiant freedom of movement the female dancers enjoyed in an age of intense sartorial restriction. For a woman to have the same freedom of movement as a man was considered quite threatening, to jump and do splits, offensive.

The screen
explodes into
can-can chaos
as dozens of
exotically
costumed female
dancers, skirts
held high, thrash
through the
Main Hall of the
Moulin Rouge
with death
defying physical
abandon.
(can-can front
row lineup,
left to right:
Schoolgirl,
Fallon King;
Arabia,
Christine Anu;
China Doll,
Natalie
Mendoza; *Nini-
Legs-in-the-Air*,
Caroline
O'Connor;
Môme Fromage,
Lara Mulcahy)

The Rakes bay at the girls' feet like lustful hounds. Zidler (*sings*): Got some dark desire? Love to play with fire? Why not let it rip? Live a little bit? Left to right: *Baby Doll*, Sue-Ellen Shook; *Historic*, Jenny Wilson; *Nini-Legs-In-the-Air*, Caroline O'Connor; *Rake*, Mark Hodge.

PHOTO BY
ELLEN VON UNWERTH

65

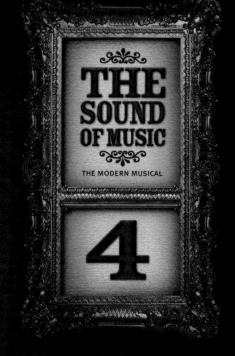

THE SOUND OF MUSIC

THE MODERN MUSICAL

4

SPECTACULAR SPECTACULAR, NO WORDS IN THE VERNACULAR CAN DESCRIBE THIS GREAT EVENT, YOU'LL BE DUMB WITH WONDERMENT, RETURNS ARE FIXED AT TEN PER CENT, YOU MUST AGREE THAT'S EXCELLENT, AND ON TOP OF YOUR FEE, YOU'LL BE INVOLVED ARTISTICALLY. SO EXCITING! THE AUDIENCE WILL STOMP AND CHEER. SO DELIGHTING! IT WILL RUN FOR FIFTY YEARS. SO EXCITING! THE AUDIENCE WILL STOMP AND CHEER. SO DELIGHTING! IT WILL RUN FOR FIFTY YEARS.

Finale - Come What May
(orchestral score)

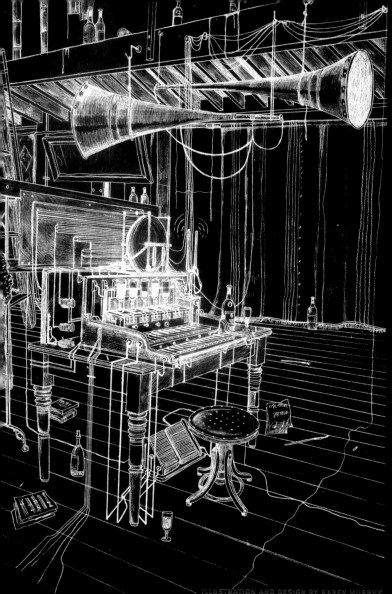

The absinthesiser is a fabricated invention. A fanciful, prototype synthesiser that uses fin de siecle Paris' most fashionable alcoholic drink – green Absinthe – as a conductor for sound. The absinthesiser came into being thanks to a weird cross-the-worlds collaboration between Moulin Rouge's Design and Music departments. In fact, at the turn of the century, people were toying around with the invention of musical instruments that used electricity. When Moulin's Design department found some pictures of a very early instrument – the electromagnetica – they used these as the basis of what eventually became the production's madcap invention, the absinthesiser.

MUSIC IS THE GREAT UNIFYING ART OF HUMANITY, ESPECIALLY MUSIC THAT TELLS A STORY.

A full break-out-into-song hasn't been around as a convention in film for quite a while. And with the golden age of the musical long gone, Luhrmann figured he would have to push the genre to the next meta level in order to reach today's cinema-savvy audiences.

Luhrmann: "Music is the great unifying art of humanity, especially music that tells a story. I agree with Pythagoras' point of view that music and matter are connected. I believe that the maths of music touches us all. If you can make music and story work together it is arguably the most powerful storytelling form."

The key in Moulin is that the actors must sing the story. Co-writer Craig Pearce explains: "As writers we've been intent on making the songs not simply an adornment but integral to the storytelling, so that there is no better way to convey a story point than with a musical number. As a result we're dealing in big strong gestures. The scenes have to build to such an extent, with the characters getting so high on the energy, that they can't do anything else but Sing!" From the outset "singing the story" must be considered to be the norm for this world. The rehearsal process laid the groundwork for setting down new rules which would help the actors find that world. Ewan McGregor: "We had four months of rehearsal to sail into that world using music to tell the story. Perhaps the most important thing about the whole rehearsal process was that by the time we started shooting when you started singing, it wasn't an issue...it had to become second nature."

Luhrmann decided from the beginning that his musical was "not about voice first and character second but about actors revealing their characters through voice." With this in mind he had to cast two people who were actors first but who could also sing.

Imitation is the highest form of flattery: orchestra members Morten Eriksen and Herbert Peppard. Photo by Sue Adler.

MUSICALLY ANYTHING GOES AS LUHRMANN'S

PALACE OF SIN OF 1899 GENERATES A BEAT AND CHOREOGRAPHY

Above: In full
flight, Nicole
was secured in
a stunt harness
and safety
wires to perform
on top of the
30ft (10.5m)
high elephant.

FILM FRAME
BY D.P. DON
MCALPINE

Of the result, Luhrmann ex-claimed in post-production, 'The extraordinary thing is that Nicole and Ewan have both become real singers. Nicole is a singer in a cabaret style like a Marlene Dietrich or a Marilyn Monroe and Ewan is a real rock singer who might easily front a rock band.' Into this parallel universe of singing and music a carefully chosen selection of well-loved musical classics have been radically restyled to advance and add resonance to Moulin's tragi-comic narrative. Luhrmann: "Once you get the audience to buy into the contract that in our world it's acceptable to sing, you need to ask — What kind of music was around at the Moulin Rouge? It was the wildest night-club of the time so it surely must have been music which would have excited the audience, pumped them up and driven them to wild, emotional heights. To convey that to our modern audience we can't actually use the music of 1899. The oompahpah brass band of Offenbach, the hardcore techno of its time would not have the same resonance and effect today. So, in our heightened Moulin Rouge film-world the music would be anything that might provoke in the contemporary audience the same kind of raw response that we imagined the visitors to the real Moulin Rouge would have felt. Be it opera, techno, rock, country and western or converted Hindi pop songs:" And to each singer, dancer, musician and even the actors, Luhrmann gave out the same challenge: "I dare you to make me say that you've gone too far." It became the template for Moulin Rouge's house style. As Musical Director Marius de Vries confirms: "Anything you can do to keep the engagement alive is fair game, so you can leap wildly from rock'n'roll to opera in one cue. If you're going to do something very, very camp like our version of 'Like A Virgin', then you have a licence to go as camp as you can. The extremity of it is a Luhrmannesque trait." Those taking up the challenge were as diverse in style as the underscore. Beck, Ozzy Osbourne, Placido Domingo, Jose Feliciano and Timbaland were amongst the many who contributed to the eclectic musical landscape.

Above all, Luhrmann's vision has entailed reinventing the musical in a style as iconically heightened as any of the classic musical spectaculars – perhaps even more so, and yet, for a contemporary audience, in a form ironic as never before.

Above: Christian, Ewan McGregor, serenades us with some of the most famous love songs of our time. PHOTO BY SUE ADLER

Right: Orchesrta member Bert Mastop awaits his cue, overseen by the omnipresent Zidler. PHOTO BY SUE ADLER

TRACK ACROSS BOOKS, PAPERS, SKETCHES, OLD PHOTOGRAPHS, STRANGE AND EXOTIC FURNITURE: A JUNKYARD OF EXPERIENCES. THE CAMERA FOLLOWS CHRISTIAN'S GAZE OUT THE WINDOW, DOWN ONTO THE DILAPIDATED MOULIN ROUGE. WE PASS SLOWLY OVER THE BOARDED-UP FACADE AND THE DECREPIT WINDMILL AND THROUGH THE DERELICT GARDEN. PUSH IN: UP THE FRONT STEPS AND INTO THE ONCE MAGNIFICENT MAIN HALL.

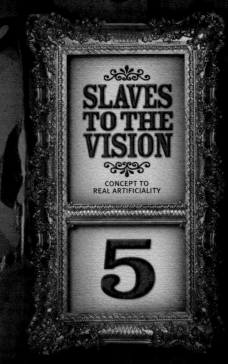

SLAVES TO THE VISION

CONCEPT TO REAL ARTIFICIALITY

5

WHEN LOVE IS FOR THE HIGHEST BIDDER THERE IS NO TRUST

Above: Draw at twenty paces. Craig and Baz write and recce in Paris, early 1998.
Right: Sketches and storyboards by Baz.

BAZ LUHRMANN | CO-WRITER

OUR STORY IS BORN OF THE ORPHEAN MYTH. THE JOURNEY OF AN IDEALISTIC YOUNG MAN WITH AN UNPARALLELED GIFT FOR SONG.

The young man travels into an underworld of lost souls in pursuit of his lost and ideal love. Having rediscovered his love he uses his gift to rescue her from this place of lost souls. But because of human failing (in our case the emotion Jealousy) he makes a fatal mistake, looks back and loses his ideal love forever. He carries on older and wiser having grown from loss. Our plot has a built-in resonance in people's memory. Ancient myths and legends have that resonance because they form the basis for our most beloved childhood stories.

Taking this story shape we inform it with the classic equation of the 19th century novel. As in Henri Murger's 'La Vie de Boheme' the sex for sale world of the courtesan/prostitute and the young bohemian sit side by side in the streets of Montmartre. Tragedy ensues when middle-class boy with romantic ideals falls in love with street girl who cannot afford them. The Argentinian says in the film "When love is for the highest bidder there is no trust, without trust, there is no love..."

BAZ LUHRMANN

76

CRAIG PEARCE

CRAIG PEARCE | CO-WRITER

This journey, like most journeys, began with ridiculous optimism.

BAZ: "A musical film based upon the Orphean myth, set in 19th century Bohemian Paris, starring the historical characters of Toulouse-Lautrec and the Moulin Rouge, but using a modern musical language. What do you think?"

CRAIG: "No problem. After *Strictly Ballroom* and *Romeo+Juliet*, that should be easy; let's knock off for an early lunch."

CUT TO 6 MONTHS LATER: 3am. Baz and I have nearly finished reading our draft to the first person we always read to, long-time collaborator and production designer, CM. CM is curled in foetal position on the floor. She appears to be asleep or in shock. It's not looking good. "The End," I say. CM hauls herself up onto an elbow. "Sorry," she says, "but starting the film with the lead character dying on a WWI battlefield is just stupid. And what sort of name is Christian?"

CUT TO 12 MONTHS LATER: "The End," I say. Baz and I have just read our new draft to a circle of trusted colleagues. Producer Martin Brown ventures cautiously: "Ah, starting the film on New Year's Eve in New York City with Christian's adopted son going off to WWII doesn't really work for me." Baz and I nod emphatically. "No, ah yes, we er...we've actually got another idea for the opening." Quickly changing tack we ask: "What about the sequence where Christian and Satine journey by hot air balloon to the secluded Chateau and are both seduced by the bisexual German Count, as drug-crazed Toulouse-Lautrec carves up his face with a razor, and Oscar Wilde and Sarah Bernhardt dance the Tango downstairs?" There are several moments of embarrassed silence. Catherine Knapman, production manager, pipes up, "I liked that bit."

CUT TO 18 MONTHS LATER: Nicole Kidman and Ewan McGregor have just read the script for the first time. Nicole smiles: "The way you two were going on I thought it was going to be terrible."

EWAN: "I think there should be more sex."

BAZ AND CRAIG: "Well, there used to be a sequence where Christian, Satine and a German Count went by hot air balloon..."

CUT TO 24 MONTHS LATER: Nicole has broken her rib. Baz's father is very sick with cancer. Shooting has been postponed.

CUT TO 25 MONTHS LATER: Finally the first day of shooting has arrived. The first shot is set up. Baz is about to call action. The Assistant Director walks on set with a mobile phone. Baz's father has died this morning.

CUT TO 30 MONTHS LATER: I see a very rough, video projection of edited sections of *Moulin Rouge*. There's no WWI battlefield, hot air balloon, German Count, adopted son, philandering uncle, betraying father, murderous money lender, Prince of Wales, attempted suicide or any other of the ridiculous, wonderful, fabulous, stupid, cowardly, brave and, ultimately just not right, places we visited on the journey. What's left is...*Moulin Rouge*. Enjoy the trip.

Below: Craig (seated bottom left) and Baz (standing top right) read a draft script, then titled *Film One*, to colleagues and collaborators in mid 1998. PHOTO BY SUE ADLER

Catherine Martin's (CM) journey as *Moulin Rouge's* Production Designer began when she accompanied Baz and co-writer Craig Pearce on a trip to write the film's synopsis in Paris. The filmmakers' aim was to find a way to reveal 19th century Paris and the Moulin Rouge as it may have felt to its audience then – sexy, energetic and bursting at the seams with all things Bohemian and modern. To create this world they researched everything from the can-can to the original Moulin Rouge architecture and interior design, to the work of Toulouse-Lautrec and the late 19th century's love affair with the kind of modern inventions that turn up in the lives of the Moulin Rouge characters.

The Moulin Rouge of the film is a conglomeration of historical fact and adaptation for storytelling clarity; elements that existed at one time or another during the first ten years of the life of the actual Moulin Rouge, as well as famous locations in Montmartre including brothels and bars. While such research was to provide the social, historical and architectural template for the heightened world of Moulin Rouge, CM's design task was to transmute these into a form provocative enough to shock and seduce a contemporary eye. "We always start pedantically, recreate precisely, then adapt and change to serve the story," explains CM. "It's about manipulating the elements extant in their world so they read now, so that a modern audience can access this period world. Baz wanted us to create a world in a style he dubbed 'real artificiality', a created Paris in which the musical of his invention would sit comfortably. A place where breaking out into song would feel natural." Baz: "One of the characteristics of the 'Red Curtain' films is the use of classic cinema references. In *Moulin Rouge* we have utilised this mechanism both in production design and cinematic style. From quoting Warner Brothers cartoons with the Bohemians to making reference to classic hair styles and costume silhouettes of the great divas of the '40s and '50s. The first moment we first see Satine she is a combination of Marilyn Monroe (*How to Marry a Millionaire*) Marlene Dietrich (*Blue Angel*), with a sprinkle of *Cabaret* and a nod to Rita Hayworth in *Gilda*. It is this constant referencing and re-referencing that we hope allows a modern audience to decode the historical setting. The ease with which the audience understands the story is crucial. In this musical we are not revealing the characters or plot slowly and invisibly but quickly and overtly."

CM's main design collaborator was Set Decorator Brigitte Broch, whilst supervising Art Director Ian Gracie headed the Art department team. Collaboration with Director of Photography Don McAlpine on the design of each set was essential. CM: "Working with Don extends the creative process. It allows me to see the sets through a lens, to see how he envisions lighting them. His huge, artistic and practical experience is invaluable in creating a set that not only looks good but can be shot effectively." Over five sound stages Catherine Martin and her vast team of art directors, assistant designers, draughts-people, graphic designers, set dressers, scenic artists, sculptors and model makers – nearly all local – meticulously manufactured the *Moulin Rouge* sets. The Moulin's infamous Elephant came up for early consideration. The Elephant was a three-storey architectural folly made of wood and papier-maché that stood in the garden of the Moulin Rouge. It contained an Arabian-themed, gentlemen-only club in its belly. Extrapolating that the Moulin Rouge doubled as a sex-for-sale, pick-up joint, the elephant was to house the sumptuous Red Room where Satine seduces Christian, mistaking the Boho poet for a Duke. But first, the gigantic mammal had to be test run. An elephant head was constructed from cane and red fabric to simulate the Red Room. From there, an elaborate plasticine Maquette became prototype for a number of different elephant sets to meet the film's various shoot requirements. A section through the elephant's forehead and back was designed at ground level for the lovers to sing atop. Another more detailed set of head, belly, and surrounding locale was constructed to

The Taj Mahal: Three detailed ivory-look models were imported from India to adorn the upholstered satin walls of the Red Room's anteroom.
PHOTO BY CHRIS GODFREY

Right: A room with a view. Miniature sets and scenic cloths combine to create the vista from the Elephant Red Room.
PHOTO BY SUE ADLER

Out de Moulin Rouge: this street exterior is an elaborate 1:4 scale model.
PHOTO BY FRANCO CARA

The Main Hall: sprung boards were laid to withstand the rigours of dancing.
PHOTO BY SUE ADLER

Full scale Elephant: When standing inside the head of the Elephant you could feel the structure sway up to 2ft (600mm). PHOTO BY SUE ADLER

Themeing: the Elephant Red Room, set for seduction. PHOTO BY SUE ADLER

Christian's Garret and Toulouse's Studio: 'L'amour fou' literally translates as 'crazy love'. PHOTO BY CHRIS GODFREY

Inside the Gothic Tower. PHOTO BY SUE ADLER

CONCEPT ILLUSTRATION BY DEBORAH RILEY

house the interior action. A full scale elephant over 30ft (10.5m) high was built on a steel frame and covered in poly-styrene to stand in the garden. Also a miniature one-fifth scale elephant was shot under snow and in disrepair.

From rough maquette to finished cons-truction, every set in the film has under-gone a similar work-shopping and testing process. CM: "It's a labour intensive process to get Baz to sign off a set. Baz's contribution to the process is vital." Although Adolphe Willette, the original designer of the Moulin Rouge, designed a themed environment (spawned by the world exhibitions and fairs of the day), modern audiences wouldn't read the themeing. For instance, the big red windmill of the Moulin's exterior referred to Montmartre as a former flour-milling district of Paris. The building had other themed facades: a Ye Olde Normandy facade, a Swiss Chalet in the garden and murals that placed you in different parts of the world. This eclectic style has been reinterpreted into themed brothel rooms like the Elephant's 'Indian' Red Room and the Gothic Tower.

Shooting required a series of one-fifth sized replicas of the Moulin Rouge and the surrounding Montmartre streetscapes.

CM explains the design aesthetic into which models and other theatrical conceits fit, "*Moulin Rouge* is a completely created world, one that we've treated in a self-consciously theatrical way. Baz wants a completeness to the world, and every design detail tries to reinforce this." CM adds that the Moulin's huge dance hall, which accommodated so much of the story's action, seemed to transcend its own theatricality, "The *Moulin Rouge* set was a very strange experience. It was standing for so long it felt like a real place. It didn't feel like it was constructed for the purposes of filmmaking. It was the Moulin Rouge."

Veteran Hollywood cinematographer Don McAlpine, who first collaborated with Baz on *Romeo+Juliet*, is quick to point out that in *Moulin Rouge* there's not a single frame that isn't heightened in some way. Realism is out the window and the slightly magical or fantastical, the super romantic is in.

McAlpine: "The last thing this film could be used for is historical reference. Everything, including the costumes which are probably the nearest to historical 'correctness,' is still only inspired by the period. There's an operatic approach by Baz and CM and I'm on the same train."

"We assume that when people saw electricity back then, they thought they were seeing the brightest, most glittering, most wonderful thing that had ever happened. We're interpreting that time into our own."

In fin-de-siècle Paris newly invented electricity – which to a modern eye would appear extremely dull – appeared dazzling. The first electric light to festoon the Moulin Rouge was a novelty drawcard opportunistically exploited by impresario Charles Zidler. Says McAlpine, "As far as the lighting is concerned, nothing can be over the top. It's heightened lighting as befits the Moulin Rouge: all glamour."

McAlpine, who stresses that the cinematography has evolved in response to script, direction and production design, credits artist Toulouse-Lautrec as an influence. "There's an underlying visual theme which CM also exploits, based on Toulouse's work. We also pay homage to some of his compositions – rascally faces in the foreground with the world happening behind them."

An unusual aspect of *Moulin Rouge* is that filming was limited to sets and reduced scale models, with virtually no location work whatsoever. If not for specific shooting strategies, the film – grand in every way – might have been diminished by the intrinsic limitations of its sets. McAlpine: "Because you can't have a new set for every scene – which is what every cinematographer would love – you have to visit the sets many times. In order to underline the story one of the many guiding principles we've had is to make the sets seem different each time we hit a new turn in the emotional journey of our characters."

With over fifty films to his credit, McAlpine confesses to employing "every trick in the book to provide the variety that Baz demands." In turn, Luhrmann likens cinematographer (and fellow Australian) McAlpine to "a great general in the field. When you're making a film it quickly moves from art to war. A war against time in which you're trying to achieve something fairly impossible with a large body of people in conditions where you can't cry foul. And Don, who will not be crushed by a challenge, is great at mustering the troops and moving them forward."

Camera, action and a really big light.
Left to right: Paul Watters, Don McAlpine, Baz Luhrmann, Steve Andrews and Chris Godfrey.

"IN *MOULIN ROUGE* THERE'S NOT A SINGLE FRAME THAT ISN'T HEIGHTENED IN SOME WAY... WHERE REALISM IS OUT THE WINDOW, THE SLIGHTLY MAGICAL OR FANTASTICAL, THE SUPER ROMANTIC IS IN."

DON MCALPINE

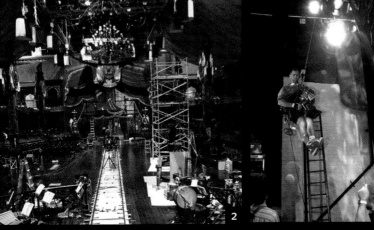

1

2

3

4

5

6

FIRST, THEY RE-THOUGHT THE CAN-CAN IN TERMS OF "A WORLD OF ENTERTAINMENT UNDER WOMEN'S DRESSES".

Costume Designers Angus Strathie and Catherine Martin (CM) began designing the 400 'period' costumes required by *Moulin Rouge's* 18 principals and 70 dancers, a year before pre-production began. Early in development CM recalls waking in horror with the realisation, "Oh my God, we're making a can-can movie, Baz! This is a hideous and revolting thing! How are we going to do it?" Both director and designers were passionately committed to re-examining the approach usually applied to the design of period costumes. Although they would base all their costume choices on rigorous historical research, they decided it was more important to convey the story, the characters and the exuberant world of the Moulin Rouge in the clearest way possible rather than with pedantic historical accuracy. This is how the costume "rules" evolved: all costume details, elements of apparel and materials had to have existed in the 19th century, but one could use them out of context. For example, Satie the avant garde composer wears sunglasses to underline his alternative rock star status, even though sunglasses in this period were only used for specific activities and were not worn as a fashion item. To give period realism to the designers' modern reinvention of 1890s Paris, costume production paid great attention to structure and finish. And whilst fabric was sent to India for expert embroidering and beading, the elaborately constructed and finished costumes were otherwise all made in a large on-site workshop by local cutters, seamstresses, dyers and milliners in Sydney (overseen by Costume Supervisor Eliza Godman). Sexy, glamorous, seductive, subversive Children of the Revolution: this is how the fin-de-siècle habitués of the Moulin thought of themselves. But such qualities are also in the eye of the beholder. CM and Strathie had to find a way of capturing the sensationalism and shock that characterised the Moulin Rouge milieu then for audiences now. First, they re-thought the can-can in terms of "a world of entertainment under women's dresses". Strathie, CM and Luhrmann came up with period versions of a series of erotic stereotypes for the can-can girls including a dominatrix (no anachronistic rubber gimp outfits, thank you), French maid, schoolgirl, cross-dresser (a sexy taboo in Paris of the day) and a baby doll. These underlined the individuality of the dancers, as originally each 19th century can-can dancer had had a speciality or a gimmick. These girls didn't dance in a kickline, identically clothed (this came later when the can-can was translated into a stage show), but rather after engaging men on the dance floor, they broke into acrobatic moves, daring each other to greater heights of physical spectacle. At the centre of the can-can is the revelation of petticoat and panties or, in the case of many 19th century dancers, the lack of underwear. In fact the very lack of underclothing was the entire reason the dance was so popular and so scandalous. The challenge for the designers was to be naughty but "nice". Strathie and CM designed a series of petticoats bordering on the rococo which revealed flashes of skin, suspender belts, coloured panties and glimpses of derrière. The can-can ruffles each underwent many processes before they were sewn onto the skirt's interior: dyeing, pleating, embroidering, ribboning, braiding. Not only this, but there were five or six layers of ruffles per skirt. It took one person a week to gather them onto a can-can skirt – and there were 30 can-can dancers. Besides being extremely beautiful artifacts, the completed can-can skirts were achingly heavy to wear. Caroline O'Connor, playing Nini Legs-in-the-Air, wore braces on her shoulders to help support the weight that strained her hips as she danced. The men's costumes were also labour-intensive. Zidler's series of "fat-suits" for which Jim Broadbent was subjected to a full body cast on which his new shape was sculptured in foam, took weeks. The period suits favoured by Christian, the Duke, Zidler and Toulouse-Lautrec (who historically loved to dress like an English lord) took over a month of hand-tailoring each. The costumes were developed in tandem with the script and customised in workshops with the actors in the year before production, with the intended result that the actors would be wearing the clothes instead of the clothes wearing them. Angus Strathie adds, "The emphasis Baz puts on design makes the world of his films seem design led, but the actors' workshops feed into the design. The designers embrace the actors' discoveries which is why there's a completeness to it all." In summation, CM flips the adage, "clothes maketh the man but actors maketh the costume."

Costume designers Catherine Martin + Angus Strathie
PHOTO BY HUGH STEWART

Left: Back view of Satine's Red Room gown with bustle. PHOTO BY SUE ADLER

THE HEIGHTENED COLOUR TEMPLATE DESIGNED BY SILVI AND SIGNORETTI INTENSIFIED AS EVERYONE REALISED JUST HOW MUCH CRAZINESS AND COLOUR THE FILM'S EXOTIC STAGING COULD STAND.

'Heightened colour for a heightened world' epitomises the work of Hair Designer Aldo Signoretti and Makeup Designer Maurizio Silvi on *Moulin Rouge* who previously have worked with such luminaries as Fellini, Visconti and Scorsese. Taking artist Toulouse-Lautrec's palette as a starting point, Moulin's exotic creatures of the night wear their hair white, pink, corn, cerise, flame-red, even dark blue. There is barely a brunette or blonde in sight. Makeup in theatrically flamboyant pursuit. Signoretti and Silvi (who first worked with Luhrmann on *Romeo+Juliet*) point out that the look of Montmartre's music hall denizens, however wild and glamorous it was deemed then, wouldn't read as such today.

In response Moulin's hair and makeup designers reinvented the original Moulin Rouge's provocative visual attitude with a look that deconstructs and transcends historical sources. Instead of Nicole Kidman's Satine looking strictly like a late 19th century Parisian courtesan, she is translated into more familiar visual terms. "A kind of diva from the 'forties with deep red hair and pearly skin," as Signoretti puts it.

Makeup and Hair Co-ordinator Lesley Vanderwalt pulled together the 60-odd hair and makeup crew who attended to lead cast, can-can dancers and the crowds of extras that make up the audience inside the Moulin Rouge. Vanderwalt (who also designed makeup on *Strictly Ballroom*) describes Luhrmann's latest production as "an amazing logistical feat in terms of hair and makeup alone."

With 85 flamboyantly coloured wigs hired or custom-made in Rome and two Australian wigmakers working into the small hours altering and mending, dressing and reblocking night after night, Luhrmann's mantra 'transportation, communication, accommodation and hair' was vindicated. Indeed, all of the lead cast (bar Ewan McGregor's Christian and John Leguizamo's Toulouse) sported a wig. In fact many of the hair and makeup transformations took hours. The Doctor, played by Gary McDonald, required three-and-a-half hours for the application of wig and facial hair each day he was required on set. In fact each actor's hair and makeup averaged three hours as hair was pin-curled, twisted under a stocking cap, topped with a wig and dressed. Constant attention had to be paid to the makeup required by lead cast like Jacek Komen's Unconscious Argentinian or Caroline O'Connor's Nini-Legs-in-the-Air as they danced through rehearsal and take after take of the production's sweaty tango.

As the shoot progressed, the colour template designed by Silvi and Signoretti intensified as everyone realised just how much craziness and colour the film's exotic staging could stand. Lesley Vanderwalt: "Subtle or 'true' period hair and makeup would have been lost in the grandness and lushness of *Moulin Rouge* sets and costumes. It would have been all sets and frocks without heads – you simply would have lost them."

Style Squad. L-R: Maurizio Silvi (Makeup Designer), Aldo Signoretti (Hair Designer), Vincenzo Mastrantonio (Makeup Artist), Caroline O'Connor (Nini-Legs-in-the-Air), Giorgio Gregorini (Hairstylist), Ferdinando Morella (Hairstylist).
PHOTO BY SUE ADLER

"*Moulin Rouge* is taking you on a ride. A roller coaster ride from beginning to end with areas of light, shade and speed changes where you least expect them. Baz and I've made *fast fast fast* our mantra but as soon as the story gets to Christian and Satine, the love story, the tragedy, we slow down," says editor Jill Bilcock of *Moulin Rouge's* cutting style.

Bilcock explains that in a Luhrmann film a multitude of events and asides are always running concurrently to the main action in a scene: "the waiters looking, the jelly on the plate wobbling" as she puts it. In *Moulin Rouge* this has spawned an equally multifaceted cutting style; one which while driving the story ever on, augments and energises the main drama by keeping an enriching eye on the comedies unfolding at the peripheries.

Referring to the musical genre, Bilcock describes *Moulin Rouge* as, "an experiment in luring back a lost audience" with Baz as the "consummate storyteller who can't resist the challenge of reconverting that audience." However she is also quick to stress that, "*Moulin Rouge* is not a musical in the old sense of the word. You shouldn't notice it's a musical because even though the cast are constantly singing, they never *stop* to sing a song. The idea has been to integrate the song into the storytelling so that there isn't a distinction, so the singing is simply another storytelling device."

Jill Bilcock has edited all of Baz's films thus far, from *Strictly Ballroom* through *Romeo+Juliet* to *Moulin Rouge*. They form a trilogy which Baz has playfully dubbed the 'Red Curtain' series. 'Red Curtain' signifying a heightened and theatrical storytelling style with a love story at its heart. Of his long-standing editor Baz comments, "No-one can cut a 'Red Curtain' film the way Jill can. She has a relentless understanding of story drive. And like me, she can't bear fatness. Jill's always looking to take the air out of scenes. She's like a canary in a coal mine. She smells gas very quickly. Jill's our bogus detector – a very harsh bogus detector – and that's her great strength."

"BAZ AND I'VE MADE FAST FAST FAST OUR MANTRA, BUT AS SOON AS THE STORY GETS TO CHRISTIAN AND SATINE, THE LOVE STORY, THE TRAGEDY, WE SLOW DOWN."

JILL BILCOCK

An Acmade ink numbering machine for coding film.
PHOTO BY KATERINA STRATOS

There are over 300 visual effects in *Moulin Rouge*. These range from minor digital corrections to long sequences (in fact two shots may be some of the longest visual effects shots in history), marrying live action to one-fifth scale models, to computer-built Parisian settings. Visual Effects Supervisor Chris Godfrey, who joined the project in pre-production, explains that the function of visual effects in *Moulin Rouge* has been primarily to extend and locate the world of Luhrmann's mythical Montmartre in the surrounding Paris of 1899.

"The visual effects have been made to underline the story rather than in the service of realism at all costs." Luhrmann continues: "We live in a world where our audience are not only aware but profoundly bored of the perfection of digital magic. Cameras move perfectly at impossible angles, reality has a beyond-real sharpness. CM and I gave Chris and the team at Animal Logic a commission that we wanted to use digital power not to create perfection but imperfection, to reproduce camera shake, deconstruct imagery and create a sense that this film was hand made. By quoting period camera moves, stock and actively pursuing cinematic imperfections of yesteryear we hoped our audience would trust more in the world that was being created. It is an oddity with this project that we spent so much money trying to make things less perfect."

A series of Photoshop collages of turn-of-the-century Paris, composited by CM's design department early in the film's development, proved inspirational. The shifting perspectives of these vistas have a theatrical quality that suits the heightened aesthetic of the rest of the film.

Working alongside Visual Effects Producer Holly Radcliffe, Godfrey supervised a large team of collaborators including Visual Effects Designer Andy Brown (Animal Logic). They built a digital Paris in Sydney based on CM's original collages.

Godfrey: "Digital shots have also solved the problem of joining disparate sets into one neighbourhood by building onto Don McAlpine's motion control footage. We've designed it so you travel over a two-dimensional Paris, which then becomes a 3-D model of the city. This city is then joined to the one-fifth scale model of the Moulin Rouge from where you make the transition into the full scale main hall. Thus with a sweeping single shot we can travel from bourgeois Paris through streets of toothless rabble and up into Christian's garret. When Don's camera couldn't get back far enough, or the set doesn't offer this or that, that's when we've used visual effects. You work right to the edges of what you can do in camera and then the visual effects build on top of that. It's an augmentation process."

"WE WANTED TO USE DIGITAL POWER NOT TO CREATE PERFECTION BUT IMPERFECTION, TO REPRODUCE CAMERA SHAKE, DECONSTRUCT IMAGERY AND CREATE A SENSE THAT THIS FILM WAS HAND MADE."

BAZ LUHRMANN

Kylie Minogue as the 'Green Fairy' assisted by our very own blue gimp, Stunt Co-ordinator Guy Norris.
PHOTO BY DANIEL SCHWARZE

1   Matte paintings are used to create the streets of Paris through which the camera flies as Baz is a ...

2   Visual Effects Supervisor Chris Godfrey reads through story-boards with Baz before testing a shot.
Photo by Sue Adler

3   A static reference plate of cardboard cut-outs was used to represent the Rakes enter in the Main Hall in this visual effects sequence.
Reference plate by Sue Adler

4   Shooting on a blue screen means people can be dropped in over created backgrounds later on.
Photo by Sue Adler

5   Story boards illustrate the visual effects.
Story boards by Christian ...

Moulin Rouge's bold collision of musical vernaculars is matched by John O'Connell's eclectic choreography. O'Connell, who also choreographed *Strictly Ballroom* and *Romeo+Juliet*, was one of the first creatives on board *Moulin Rouge.* Even as Baz and Craig were dreaming the script, he was researching musicals and the can-can, as he attests:

"I began by researching the old musicals: the Ritz Brothers who were like a dancing version of the Marx Bros, Maurice Chevalier's first music movie in Hollywood, Folies Bergère. When you see that old stuff you think they were on something, they were crazy. What inspired me was the wit and imagination, a playfulness and joy that disappeared with later musicals. I also looked at hundreds of Bollywood movies which to me capture the essence of forties and fifties Hollywood musicals, the fun. And of course, I researched the can-can which has been seen so many times we had to find a way to bring a freshness and energy. In fact, when they originally did the can-can what was shocking was less that they lifted up their skirts and more that they had such freedom of movement."

O'Connell's wildly diverse choreography for *Moulin* pays witty homage to iconic musical and dance styles: from Bollywood for the Hindu 'Spectacular Spectacular' to the Busby Berkeley musicals for the culmination of Ewan McGregor's 'Your Song', to Hello Dolly for the Hollywood style kicklines of 'Like a Virgin'.

Ranging far beyond Paris 1899, the Moulin Rouge melange of dance styles nevertheless eschews obviously anachronistic or out-of-character movements. There are no grinding pelvises for the male tango dancers for instance. Whereas the women, by dint of their respective professions – actresses, prostitutes and erotic dancers – have more licence.

Choreographing Ewan and Nicole, the support leads, 60 dancers, 10 acrobats and up to 300 extras, O'Connell's huge dance numbers and smaller-scale moves add maximum resonance – dark, witty, erotic, playful – to the story. Look for the Unconscious Argentinian and Nini Legs-in-the-Air's tango as it forms a dark parallel to the thwarted lovers' triangle of Satine, Christian and the Duke (or to put it another way, to *Moulin's* other great triangle: Sex, Art and Commerce).

Of O'Connell himself Luhrmann comments, "In a very practical sense he has an unparalleled genius for a choreographic style that once flourished, a choreography which is clever, silly and thoroughly inventive."

"WHEN THEY ORIGINALLY DID THE CAN-CAN WHAT WAS SHOCKING WAS LESS THAT THEY LIFTED UP THEIR SKIRTS AND MORE THAT THEY HAD FREEDOM OF MOVEMENT."

JOHN O'CONNELL

Rehearsals: Sheds at Fox Studios were converted into dance studios with mirrored walls and sprung floors.
PHOTO BY SUE ADLER

One of the ultimate challenges for the filmmakers on *Moulin Rouge* has been making the full break-out-into-song musical genre work technically and expressively for story, actors and audience. Luhrmann: "The device of contemporary music set against a period setting was standard fare in the heyday of the musical. Even though the film 'Meet me in St Louis' is set in 1900, Judy Garland sings 'The Trolley Song', a popular, contemporary radio hit of the 1940s. Usually the musical numbers were already familiar to the audience, either by the virtue of having been radio hits or as in the case of 'No Business like Show Business' or 'White Christmas' were favourites used in more than one production, allowing the audience to have an immediate emotional connection to these songs. This was the genesis of the following device: Christian was to channel the great popular tunes of the 20th century underlining the character's near-genius and poetic musical abilities. We also wanted to avoid the traditional musical form where the music is from one voice, i.e. one composer. We wanted the score to be as eclectic as the *Romeo+Juliet* sound track, moving through many styles from opera, electronica to pop and rock and to work with dozens of musical collaborators, composers, producers, arrangers, musicians and performers. To bring these talents together we created a core musical team formed by Musical Director Marius de Vries, Composer Craig Armstrong, Arranger Chris Elliot, Music Supervisor Anton Monsted, Music Programmer/Producer Josh Abrahams and Composer/Arranger Steve Hitchcock."

The musical storytelling of the piece and the writing of the script developed in parallel; one fed the other until the script became a combination of conventional film script, and musical storytelling. With the songs as crucial storytelling devices, Anton Monsted and Josh Abrahams began supplying writers Luhrmann and Craig Pearce with song lists. Monsted recalls: "The songs were to serve what Luhrmann and Pearce called STAFs: 'Scenes That Are Fundamental'. Each STAF demanded a song cue that would work to illustrate the story in a way dialogue or regular action could not. Songs often had to work as sung speech, as in Christian's 'poems'. The idea was to combine story with song to create a third meaning. A lot of final song choices like 'Like A Virgin' are witty, lateral ideas suggestive of another level of meaning within the film."

The evolution of every musical number took several years. Each song used in the film had already been workshopped with the actors, rehearsed, and recorded by the time it was shot. Advances in digital recording technology meant the process of drafting and redrafting could continue all the way through the show and across three continents. It also meant that recording vocals and instruments no longer required a strict studio environment. Next, the filmmakers asked the question – When our characters start singing does it feel awkward? To solve this, several options were investigated to ensure the best performance. Either to pre-record the vocal track so that actors lip sync to their own performance or having performers singing live on set to a keyboard accompaniment (or sometimes a backing or guide track). Like a concert performance, the pianist could then follow the emotional direction the singer wished to take the song on the day, giving a less mechanical, and more in-the-moment performance. Musical Director de Vries comments "It's a constant search for extremity. Every emotional envelope, you try and push it as far as you can. You can subvert the history of the genre you're working in but you have to come to terms with it one way or another. By adopting a perpetually eclectic approach – as contemporary and as retro as we can make it – I believe that we're creating something that's quite different from what's been done with a musical before." Composer Craig Armstrong adds, "Almost nothing is exactly what it seems at the start, everything can be mutated. Songs dissolve and become part of the score only to reappear in different form. I think that's a very Baz Luhrmann thing to do, to ask – How far can you take this version? To explore a piece of music right to the very end."

"IT'S A CONSTANT SEARCH FOR EXTREMITY. EVERY EMOTIONAL ENVELOPE, YOU TRY AND PUSH IT AS FAR AS YOU CAN."

MARIUS DE VRIES

The ever-changing track list.
PHOTO BY BRANCO GAICA

1. Baz with Conductor Christopher Gordon and Director of Music Anton Monsted in the control room of 301 Studios, Sydney.
PHOTO BY DAMIEN PLEMMING

2. Christopher Gordon conducting a children's choir to accompany Bono on the soundtrack to 'Dance Across the Sky'.
PHOTO BY DAMIEN PLEMMING

3. Recording the orchestra.
PHOTO BY DAMIEN PLEMMING

4. Marius mixes at Soundfirm in Sydney.
PHOTO BY ANNA FALVEY

5. Studio kitchen at a recording session with young Josh Nathan-Kazis.
PHOTO BY ANNA FALVEY

6. Suited boys get down.
PHOTO BY SUE ADLER

7. Ewan McGregor rocks.
PHOTO BY SUE STUMPF GREENE

8. Orchestral recording.

9. Marius orchestra.
PHOTO BY SUE ADLER

"WE MADE A DECISION AT A CERTAIN POINT, TO REALISE EVERY ASPECT OF THE SHOW ON STUDIO STAGES."

MARTIN BROWN

Martin Brown (PRODUCER)

We made a decision at a certain point, to realise every aspect of the show on studio stages. It's reminiscent, in a way, of studio films of the 1940s where westerns gave you a guy with a fake campfire and a backdrop vista. It's intentionally theatrical. Baz calls it 'real artificiality', which means you have to enter into a contract with the film whereby you're prepared to suspend your disbelief. Believability comes from the two leads' love story: that's what you connect to emotionally. Baz calls it 'wide awake cinema'.

"THE STRAIT BETWEEN COMMERCE AND ART IS NARROW AND NEVER EASY TO NAVIGATE..."

BAZ LUHRMANN

Baz Luhrmann (PRODUCER)

As our character Audrey, the writer, used to say in one of the early drafts of the script: "The strait between commerce and art is narrow and never easy to navigate..." This has been true with all our Red Curtain films. Films that attempt to break new ground are by their very nature perceived as high risk. As always we have tried to extend our finances far beyond their earthly limits. The challenge is to realise a complicated project within economic limitations. This challenge is not new to us. It has forced us to be more inventive in the way in which we do things. While we do not allow these constraints to dictate our creativity it compels us to find lateral solutions to solve budgetary problems. I would argue that anyone could make something remarkable if allowed infinite funding and time. The reality for all of us though is that there is a set amount of time and a set amount of funds for each project. Creativity is about transcending these immutable things; even Michelangelo had to eventually stop painting the Sistine Chapel.

"THEY CREATE A WORLD. THEY GO WAY OVER THE TOP BUT YOU BUY IT, YOU BUY INTO IT."

FRED BARON

Fred Baron (PRODUCER)

The world loves a musical. For so many people it was their first film experience. Baz has taken this classic form and has remixed it to create a new cocktail, a new form. In the traditional Hollywood musical, the actor breaks into song and you know it's pre-recorded. Our actors are doing something very daring: singing live on camera. Even though *Moulin Rouge* pays its own style of homage to classic-type musical numbers, the audience never feels, "Oh, it's a production number. Okay, it's a musical." What Baz is trying to create is the feeling that the singing is the acting, that you're not leaving the world of the story. Baz is trying to draw you inside the characters so that their inner voice is a musical voice.

The world of Baz and CM is operatic in tone, whether it's a musical or Shakespeare. They create a world. They go way over the top but you buy it, you buy into it.

Painter Linda Sang finishes just in the nick of time.
PHOTO BY SUE ADLER

Do as I say and as I do. Baz directs Deobia Oparei as the Hindu God.

Lighting, costume and camera checks on the set of 'Dance Across the Sky'.

Baz and Nicole enjoy the view.

Producer Fred Baron holding the original maquette of the elephant, against the backdrop of the full size elephant.

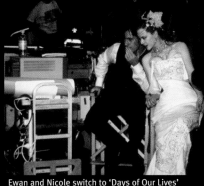
Ewan McGregor, Jacek Komen, Nicole Kidman and Matthew Whittet jam to some funky recorder.

"It's a wrap!" Baz is overjoyed.

Cha-Cha (John O'Connell) and Kiruna Stamell (Petite Princesse) in discussion.

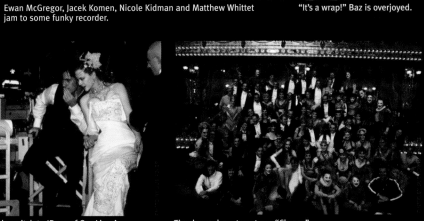
Ewan and Nicole switch to 'Days of Our Lives' while the director isn't looking.

The dance department say "Cheese".

Trial and error. John Leguizamo in the Toulouse-Lautrec walking machine.

Nicole Kidman between takes on the set of 'Black Diamonds'.

Rounding up the extras.

Department heads meet on every new set the night before shooting. Left to right: Paul Watters, Catherine Martin, Steve Andrews, Patrick McArdle, Ian Gracie, Don McAlpine, Martin Brown, Catherine Knapman, Steve Mathis and Simon Lee.

THE MOULIN ROUGE WAS ESSENTIALLY AN EROTIC AND DECADENT WORLD OF SENSUALITY AND SEX-FOR-SALE. UNWERTH'S SEXY DISTINCTIVE STYLE CAPTURES THE DEBAUCHED AND EROTIC PHYSICALITY OF THE CAN-CAN, AS WELL AS THE BACCHANALIAN GLAMOUR OF THE STARS OF THE *MOULIN ROUGE.*

ELLEN VON UNWERTH

GUEST PHOTOGRAPHER

6

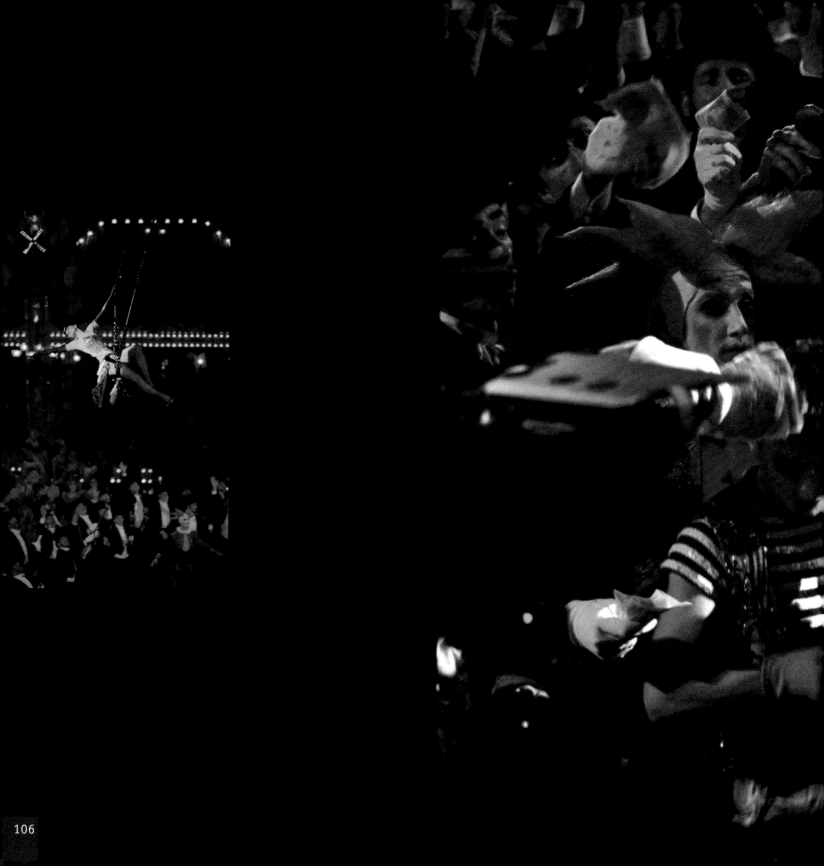

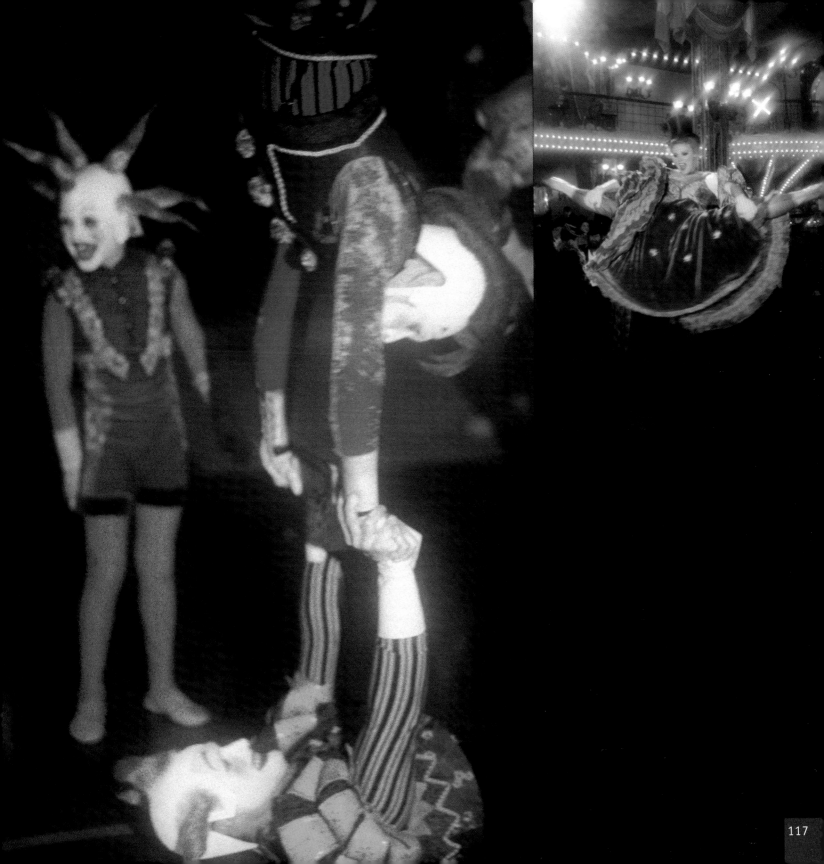

Twins! Ewan McGregor and Ellen von Unwerth (left). Richard Roxburgh, Jim Broadbent and Ewan McGregor learn a thing or two from Ellen's book 'Couples' (right).

The multi talented Ewan McGregor. Bottom right: "This one's for you David La Chapelle!"

The poet and his muse. Ewan McGregor and Nicole Kidman.

The 'Sparkling Diamond' Satine. Nicole Kidman.

She was the star of the Moulin Rouge and she sold her love to men. Satine commands the floor.

L to R: Ewan Mcgregor with the flour miller's wife; Môme Fromage (Lara Mulcahy) with Rakes (Deon Nuku and Troy Phillips); a walk in the park (Ewan McGregor), and resident bon vivant Toulouse-Lautrec (John Leguizamo).

In full swing. 'Don't say you can't, can't, can't because you can, can, can!' featuring Nini-Legs-in-the-Air (Caroline O'Connor).

Absinthe in the afternoon with the Siamese Twins (Maya and Nandy McLean), and with Chocolat (Deobia Oparei).

L to R: Nini (Caroline O'Connor); Skirts on fire; Ta dah! Zidler (Jim Broadbent) and his Diamond Dogs.

L to R: Can-can chaos! Le Petomane (Keith Robinson); La Cha-u-kao (Pina Conti); Antoinette (Fleur Denny); Tabasco Brothers (Jordan Ashton, Shaun Holloway, Chris Mayhew); High Kick (Wendy McMahon).

L to R: Nini and Toulouse (John Leguizamo and Caroline O'Connor); Tabasco Brother Clown (Adrien Jansseno) and Baby Doll (Sue-Ellen Shook) with Rake (Nathan Wright).

L to R: Partners in crime Chocolat (Deobia Oparei) and Petite Princess (Kiruna Stammell); comedy & cabaret (Lara Mulcahy, Natalie Mendoza, Kiruna Stammell); the can-can (Natalie Mendoza); and Jim Broadbent air-conditions his fat suit.

MARK IS KNOWN FOR HER INSIGHTFUL, BEAUTIFUL AND OFTEN UNNERVING PICTURES OF THE FRINGES OF CONVENTIONAL SOCIETY. HER CELEBRATED WORK IN THE BIZARRE CIRCUS UNDER-WORLD OF INDIA MADE IT SEEM PARTICULARLY APPROPRIATE FOR HER TO RECORD IN A SERIES OF REMARKABLE IMAGES THE DECADENT AND DISTURBING THEATRICAL WORLD OF THE *MOULIN ROUGE*.

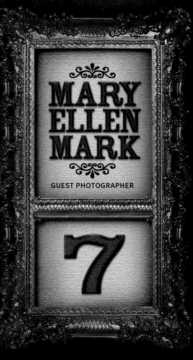

MARY ELLEN MARK

GUEST PHOTOGRAPHER

7

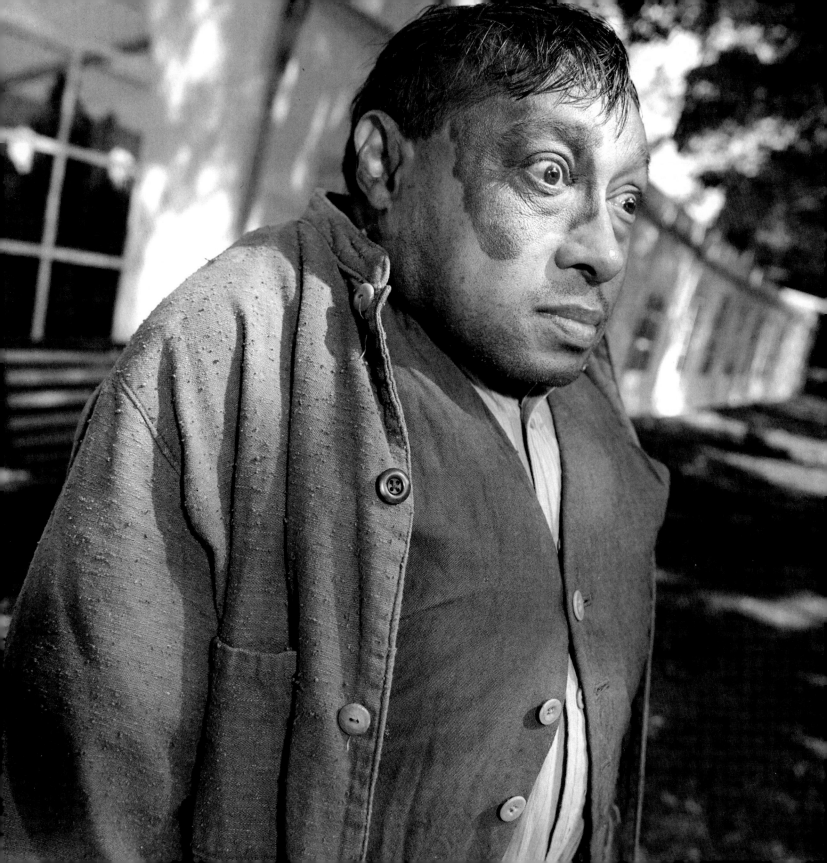

Left: Zidler with his Merry Moulin Band. (L-R: Caroline O'Connor, Keith Robinson, Jim Broadbent, Natalie Mendoza, Lara Mulcahy.) Right: Nini-Legs-in-the-Air (Caroline O'Connor).

Right: Assistant Director Paul Sullivan drops into the elephant unannounced. Left: Illustrated men (L-R: Luis Anivitti and 'Piercer' Paul Anderson).

Left: Le Petomane (Keith Robinson, left) in a flatulent moment with Petite Princesse (Kiruna Stammell). Right: a family affair (left to right: Melanie and Peta Stammell).

A live mermaid was one of the attractions dreamed up for the Garden's sideshow. Right: Disco Sally (Lorna Wright) hurries up and waits.

Culture clash. The Moulin Rouge cut across traditional social barriers. (Front row, left to right: Patrick Gleeson, Brian Fellow and 'Piercer' Paul Anderson).

Left: The Degas Ballerinas (L-R: Tony Anderson, Alan Lloyd, Herbert de Longueville and Peter Javelin). Right: Dandy with dog.

Toulouse (John Leguizamo): "You see me as a drunken vice-ridden gnome, whose only friends are pimps and the girls of brothels, but I know about art and love, if only because I long for it with every fibre of my being."

Zidler's (Jim Broadbent, left) can-can whores are based on fetish stereotypes, of which China Doll (Natalie Mendoza, right) is the perfect example.

Toulouse-Lautrec (John Leguizamo) with the Bohos (left to right) the Doctor (Garry McDonald), Satie (Matthew Whittet) and the Unconscious Argentinian (Jacek Komen).

CUT TO: One of the Toothless Rabble (right: Michael Tauro) and Left

CELEBRATED PORTRAIT PHOTOGRAPHER DOUGLAS KIRKLAND HAS PHOTOGRAPHED SOME OF THE GREATEST FEMALE ICONS OF OUR TIME, FROM MARILYN MONROE, TO COCO CHANEL AND THE SINGLE TEAR OF JUDY GARLAND. THUS, IT SEEMS APPROPRIATE FOR HIM TO TURN HIS LENS ON A MODERN DIVA — SATINE (NICOLE KIDMAN), THE SPARKLING DIAMOND, SURROUNDED BY AN ICONIC CAST OF CHARACTERS FROM OUR *MOULIN ROUGE*.

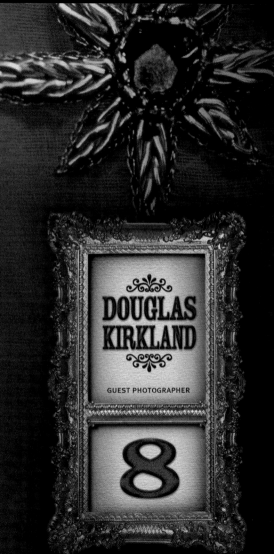

DOUGLAS KIRKLAND

GUEST PHOTOGRAPHER

8

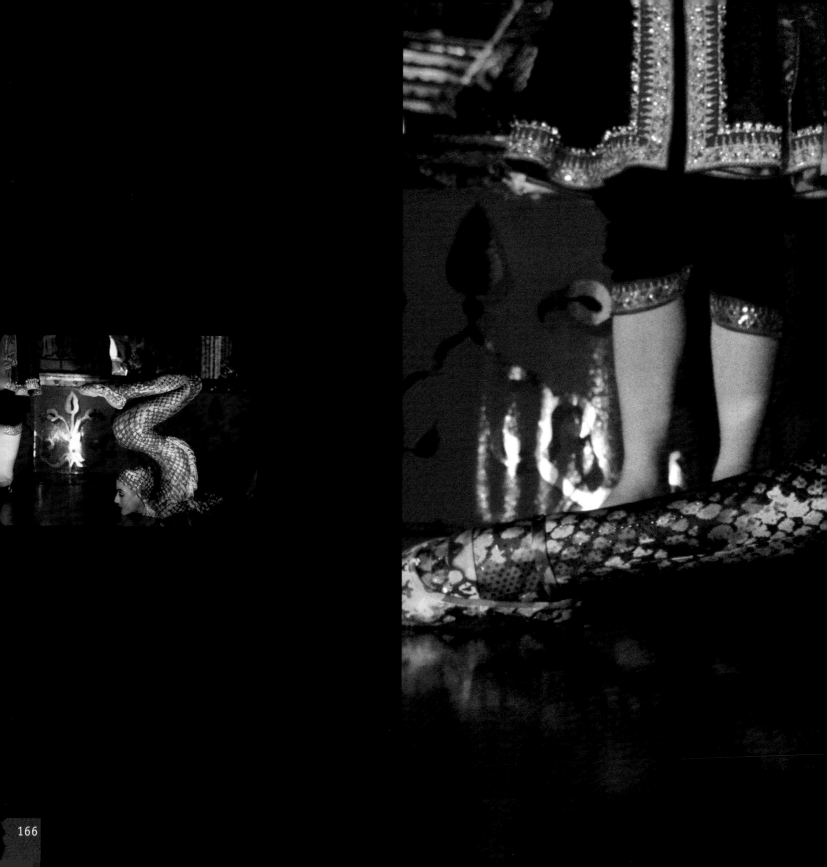

Ewan McGregor (left), Baz Luhrmann and Nicole Kidman (right). All hail the video split.

Satine (Nicole Kidman) as the Hindu Courtesan who sacrifices her love for a Penniless Sitar Player saving the kingdom from the Evil Maharaja.

Materials for Nicole Kidman's Hindu Courtesan costume were shipped from India to Sydney where artisans converted them into elaborate headdresses and costumes.

Dance Across the Skies - Satine (Nicole Kidman) and Christian (Ewan McGregor) serenaded by the moon, trip the light fantastic.

The Hindu: Hollywood goes Bollywood.

Don McAlpine (left) and Baz Luhrmann (right); a partnership in problem solving.

INTERIOR MOULIN ROUGE. STAGE. NIGHT. (ACT 1 SET): The chorus reaches its diabolically shattering climax. The Hindu Gods clasp the diamonds around Satine's neck. The necklace explodes into a trillion spots of light.

INTERIOR MOULIN ROUGE. ON STAGE. NIGHT: Nini-Legs-in-the-Air (Caroline O'Connor, left) gives a whole new meaning to her name. An explosion reveals Zidler (Jim Broadbent) as the Evil Maharaja., right).

Diamond Dogs Môme Fromage (Lara Mulcahy, left) and China Doll (Natalie Mendoza, right) flank the Hindu God (Deobia Oparei).

Attention to detail: a contortionist (Pina Conti) playing a snake is charmed from her basket by the Penniless Sitar Player.

Satine (Nicole Kidman) in the garden: a set which took six months to build, stood for only three days of filming and was demolished in under 24 hours.

TWENTIETH CENTURY FOX PRESENTS A BAZMARK PRODUCTION

NICOLE KIDMAN · EWAN McGREGOR · "MOULIN ROUGE" · JOHN LEGUIZAMO · JIM BROADBENT · RICHARD ROXBURGH

ORIGINAL SCORE BY CRAIG ARMSTRONG · MUSIC DIRECTOR MARIUS DeVRIES · CHOREOGRAPHY JOHN O'CONNELL · CO-PRODUCER CATHERINE KNAPMAN · EDITED BY JILL BILCOCK

PRODUCTION DESIGNED BY CATHERINE MARTIN · DIRECTOR OF PHOTOGRAPHY DONALD M. McALPINE, ACS/ASC · PRODUCED BY MARTIN BROWN · BAZ LUHRMANN · FRED BARON

PG-13 PARENTS STRONGLY CAUTIONED ⊛
Some Material May Be Inappropriate for Children Under 13
Sexual Content

SOUNDTRACK AVAILABLE ON INTERSCOPE RECORDS

WRITTEN BY BAZ LUHRMANN & CRAIG PEARCE · DIRECTED BY BAZ LUHRMANN

DOLBY
IN SELECTED THEATRES

20th CENTURY FOX

© 2001 TWENTIETH CENTURY FOX

www.clubmoulinrouge.com

BOOK PRODUCED BY BAZMARK DESIGN

KEY DESIGNERS: Katerina Stratos, Silvana Azzi and Gretta Kool.
ADDITIONAL DESIGN: Alexandra Bolton, Nikki Di Falco, Melissa Silk, Todd Southeren and Ben Walsh.

PHOTOGRAPHY: Sue Adler
GUEST PHOTOGRAPHERS: Douglas Kirkland (pp 149-171) Mary Ellen Mark (pp 125-147) Ellen von Unwerth (pp 99-123)
ADDITIONAL PHOTOGRAPHY: Branco Gaica, Chris Godfrey, Don McAlpine, Hugh Stewart,
Damien Plemming, Daniel Schwarze and Katerina Stratos.
IMAGES ON P50-55: By arrangement with Bibliothèque nationale de France, Paris.

WRITER: Miro Bilbrough
ADDITIONAL TEXT AND CAPTIONS: Sarah Salkild and Philip Drake
PRODUCTION TEAM: Philip Drake, Sarah Salkild, Brooke Flint and Rebecca Perkins

WITH SPECIAL THANKS TO: Everyone at Bazmark, Bob Harper, Jeffrey Godsic, Carol Sewell and Steve Newman;
Mr. Balos and the team at Balos Book Binding; Sarah Fletcher at Digital Masters; Petra Kell at Show-Ads;
Joy Willis at Phoenix Asia Pacific; Mark, John and Chris at Colours; Angus Martin, Emily O'Connell, Claire Macken,
Sonoma Message, Edweana Wenkart, Tania Burkett, Naomi Cox, Lisa Schremmer, David Ratner, Hinemihi P. Kingi.

CREATIVE DIRECTORS: Baz Luhrmann and Catherine Martin